Montessori Classroom Lesson Plans:

January

History/Time/South America

By

Robin Norgren, M.A.

"The greatest gifts we can give our children are the roots of responsibility and the wings of independence."

-Maria Montessori

Lessons are given individually or as a small group according to the needs and abilities of the children, the particular work or personal or school philosophy.

Each day, the children are allowed an uninterrupted work period where they can work undisturbed and receive one on one lessons. Begin the year with a short work time and increase it gradually to 3 hours. The work period is filled with movement. A piece of work may involve returning to the shelf several times. This is the movement Dr. Montessori intentionally built into the lessons. The children are allowed freedom to walk around while finding the next material to work with and have the option of a quiet place such as a reading corner for a quiet break. The extended/outside classroom is accessible from the inside classroom and offer activities such as woodworking and gardening.

The times given for circle, group and work periods are a sample schedule to be adapted to your school's routine and the children's needs. Present a circle (or not) according to the natural flow of the classroom, respecting the uninterrupted work period and modifying them according to the changing interests and the needs of the children. Be in the moment. Integrate other ideas and subjects of interest to you and the children. Having a genuine joy and enthusiasm for the topic of study while being natural and spontaneous is an integral element of Montessori.

Montessori taught that the first job of the teacher is to prepare an environment where the child can teach herself and develop self-discipline. The classroom and its materials, plants, and animals are enthusiastically cared for by the children. Perhaps the most difficult tenet the

Montessori classroom director is asked to embody is to become invisible enough to allow this to occur.

A Discussion about your Language Album

In the September, October and November Guides, all letters were introduced. Over the next month, you will begin to gather data based on the introduction of all letters to your students. Some students will not show much interest. Many of your 3-year olds may spend most of their time in Practical Life and Sensorial or in your Outdoor Environment. Because you will continue to build vocabulary and awareness of sound through singing, conversations and lessons given, the students will continue to build interest for your language area.

In the meantime, focus can shift to those students that have increased interest in learning their letters, building letter sound awareness and building stamina to sound out words and start to read. In my environment, I have a sound table where I can work with the child one on one and gauge where each one is at and track the growth in this area. Each one has a Sound Book that has a page with each one of the lowercase letters listed on the page – place them in the book in random order rather than "a, b, c" order. I will sit with a child and go through the book until we have three sounds that the child is unaware of. I take those 3 letters and do a three-period lesson with the sandpaper letters. I also have a box of sand that I use to have them trace the letters in the sand. Finally, I have a small booklet labeled "secret message" that I send home with the three-letter sound that I want the child to work on at home. I proceed in this way until the child has about 90% grasp of the letter sounds. Then I begin to transition the child into the AMS Language system of Pink, Blue and Green reading system and couple that with BOB books.

Montessori Basics: Pink, Blue, and Green Series

The Pink, Blue, and Green Series work is an integral part of Montessori language. Many people have questions about these materials, though. They don't seem quite as self-explanatory as other common Montessori work. There's a lot to know about the history and usage of these materials – so read on for more info!

When Maria Montessori began working with the children in the first Casa dei Bambini (Children's House), she gave them sandpaper letters to trace while saying the correct sound. She didn't do any specific work in the area of reading, but almost effortlessly, the children began to read. Italian is a very phonetic language (words are spelled the way they sound), and once the children knew the sounds, they could read.

After the Montessori method was brought to the United States in the 1920s, it was clear that another approach was needed to teach reading and writing in English. While there are many phonetically spelled words in English, there are even more that use "phonemes"; that is, groups of letters that create distinct sounds when combined. For instance, "ough" can make several sounds, as in "through" or "bough". These sounds need to be memorized; they can't be sounded out phonetically.

The Pink, Blue, and Green Series materials were developed to meet that need. They break down the essentials of English phonics into three groups: short vowel sounds, consonant blends, and phonetic combinations. By moving through these materials in order, a child can easily master the art of reading and writing in English.

The Pink Series materials are where it all begins. Pink Series words consist of three letters: a beginning and ending consonant, and a vowel in the middle. All the vowel sounds in this series are short vowels: "a" as in "c**a**t"; "e" as in "b**e**d", "i" as in "p**i**g", "o" as in "h**o**t", and "u" as in "b**u**s". The letter "y" is not included in this grouping.

After mastering the Pink Series, the child is ready to move to Blue Series words. These words consist of consonant blends (at the beginning or end of the word, or both), and a short vowel sound. Examples would include "flag", "mend", and "clock". There are about 20 different blends, if you include doubles like "ll" and "ss". The child may work on this step for quite a while, as there are hundreds of words that fit into this scheme (see picture for an example of Blue Series matching cards).

Once the Blue Series words have been mastered (essentially, that means the child is familiar with all the blends and can spell most Blue Series Words), they are ready for Green Series. The Green Series is where reading fluency really begins, as the child now has the keys to unlock the inconsistencies and idiosyncrasies of the English language.

The Green Series words consist of all the major phonemes, for example: "ai", "ou", "ie", and "ow". It also includes vowel combinations with a consonant in the middle, like "a_e" or "i_e" where the "_" is a consonant. These would be words like "c**a**k**e**" or "m**ice** ". It includes silent letters, hard and soft letters, and many other difficult spellings and reading challenges. There are about 40-50 different sound combinations in this group.

There is a huge variety of Pink, Blue, and Green Series work. Common ones include matching cards, rhyming cards, using the movable alphabet to spell words, cards with lists of words for spelling or reading practice, and word cards with matching objects. Materials differ by classroom and teacher and most Montessori companies have their own personalized sets of materials that are all slightly different.

Pink, Blue, and Green Series materials are easy to make at home; for suggestions, check out this post:

What Can You Do with the Language Basics?

The great thing is, most Montessori materials have multiple uses for different age groups. So, here are a few things you can do with the Language Basics:

Beginning set up for 6-9 language:

Pink, blue, & green series materials
Word study materials
Movable alphabet

The Pink, Blue, & Green series materials should include word lists or spelling cards, and pictures and objects of Pink, Blue, & Green series words. Pictures can be photos, clipart, or even cut out of books or magazines. Objects can be easily found around the house or classroom; here's some suggestions:

Pink Objects
pen
nut
jet (toy airplane)
bag (small gift bag)
cup
bus
map (print a small one off the internet & laminate)
peg (from lite brite)
rug (a small oval of fabric)
top (toy that spins)
box (small jewelry box)
animals from a farm or play set: cat, dog, fox

Blue Objects:
ball
bell

block (wooden toy)
brush (paint or hair)
clip (paper clip)
rock
flag
ring
shell
sock & shoe from a doll

Green Objects:
spool
leaf
rose
dime
cube (square block)
bead
soap (hotel-sized bar)
seed
globe

Okay, now that you've assembled some Pink, Blue, & Green materials, you need a movable alphabet. Those can be easily stored in a plastic tackle box (find that at a craft or hobby store).

The child can use the objects and/or pictures to spell words, rhyme words, and write stories – all with the movable alphabet. Have them take all the objects from one set, put them on their rug, and spell each one out with the movable alphabet. Or, choose one object, spell it, and then think of 2-3 words that rhyme with it and spell those out too. Or, have the child spell the color of each object.

The word lists or spelling cards can be used as story starters, spelling tests (both written and oral), spelling bees, and alphabetization practice. Pink, Blue, and

Green series words can also be looked up in the dictionary for dictionary practice.

Word Study materials should include title cards that say "masculine/feminine", "short vowel/long vowel", "person/place/thing", and "singular/plural". The child can use the movable alphabet or slips of scrap paper to write appropriate words for each category. Other word study cards include compound word matching, homophones, prefix/suffix, and contractions.

These materials – and the variations contained within – could easily be used for the first few months of school for 6-9-year olds. Stories written with the movable alphabet could be written on paper in cursive by older students; either they could turn it into cursive on their own, or use a cursive movable alphabet to start with (naturally the difficulty of the story itself will increase as the child's age increases)

Handwriting

I highly recommend coupling a program called "Handwriting Without Tears" with your curriculum. My director paid for the Lead Teachers to go through the course. They are usually offered ½ day or full day. You are given all the materials to use in the classroom setting. What I loved about the course is that it broke uppercase and lowercase letters into 4 components: long lines, short lines, big curves, little curves. The handwriting of the students changed DRAMATICALLY using these simple cues and the wood shapes that come with the workshop. I would offer group lessons with chalkboards and I can easily say that this activity was one of the high points of the child's day.

CLICK HERE for more information

Calendar Time/Star Student of the Week

The prior guides introduced the main components of a traditional calendar time:

- Days of the week
- Months of the year
- Weather

You may want to consider adding this your group time. This is a kindergarten requirement in many States.

You may also want to consider a *"Student of the Week"* option where a child works at home on a list of questions and the family gathers pictures and creates a poster presentation of the information. Each day the child has an opportunity to answer 1-2 questions a day at your groups time and talk about the picture that represents that part of his/her history. This incorporates many of the story telling lessons you find in your Language Album. It also allows for new friends to be made based on common interests and shared backgrounds/ideas/traditions.

CLICK HERE for the kit that I have created.

Geography Home Based Projects

I LOVE finding ways to extend what we learn in the classroom to home conversations and field trips and travel. I find that Geography is a fantastic way to spark this interest. Many children have the opportunity to travel. Some children have been born or have lived in other countries, even on other continents. This is the opportunity to bring world connectedness to the classroom.

The beginning of the month I will send home a newsletter with some suggestions based on the continent we will study. This is simply a starting point and many of the ideas will be sparked when I use the kits that I have made for each continent. The child can bring in artifacts from their family's belongings or put together an age appropriate presentation (no more than 5 minutes) to present in class. If a parent would like to handle the presentation, I suggest that you offer some parameters because you will find many parents will create a presentation appropriate for ADULTS not preschool children.

When the child brings something to share, depending on the age of the child, I will ask her/him to also gather three facts to share with the group.

North America kit

South America Kit

Topics We Introduce in January:

South America

Time

Handwriting

Calendar Time

Home based Projects for Continent Works

Letter Writing

Frogs

Monkeys

Shadows

Our State

Student of the Week

SPECIAL DATES DURING JANUARY

January 1 ---New Year's Day
January 6 ---Epiphany
January 7 -------------------------------Orthodox Christmas Day
January 14------------------------------------Orthodox New Year
January 20-------Martin Luther King, Jr. Day/Civil Rights Day
January 21------------------------------------TuBishvat/Tu B'Shevat

January Book List

New Year's

Shanté Keys and the New Year's Peas by Gail Piernas-Davenpor, illustrated by Marion Eldridge
The Stars Will Still Shine by Cynthia Rylant, illustrated by Tiphanie Beeke.
Every Month Is a New Year: Celebrations Around the World by Marilyn Singer.
Happy New Year, Spot! by Eric Hill
P. Bear's New Year's Party: A Counting Book by Owen Paul Lewis
Squirrel's New Year's Resolution by Pat Miller
Happy New Year Everywhere! by Arlene Erlbach
The Night Before New Year's by Natalie Wing

Lunar/Chinese New Year

Bringing in the New Year by Grace Lin
Sam and the Lucky Money by Karen Chinn
Rabbit's Gift by George Shannon
The Emperor and the Kite by Jane Yolen
The Seven Chinese Sisters by Kathy Tucker
The Seven Chinese Brothers by Margaret Mahy
King Pom and the Fox by Jessica Souhami
Two of Everything by Lily Toy Hong

Tu B'Shevat Books

Happy Birthday Tree! by Madelyn Rosenberg, illustrated by Jana Christy
Netta and Her Plant by Ellie B. Gellman, illustrated by Natascia Ugliano

Time

Telling the Time by Rupert Matthews
The Man Who Made Time Travel by Kathryn Lasky
About Time: A First Look at Time and Clocks by Bruce Kocsielniak
It's About Time by Pascale Estellon
Just a Second by Steve Jenkins
A Second is a Hiccup by Hazel Hutchins
Time is When by Beth Gleick
All in a Day by Cynthia Rylant
The Very Hungry Caterpillar by Eric Carle
Four Seasons Make a Year by Anne Rockwell
As an Oak Tree Grows by G. Brian Karas
Big Time Bears by Stephen Krensky.
All About Time by Andre Verdet
Winnie the Pooh Tells Time inspired by A.A. Milne
Game Time by Stuart Murphy
I.Q., It's Time by Mary Ann Fraser
Cluck O'Clock by Kes Gray
The Grouchy Ladybug by Eric Carle
Telling Time by Jules Older
The Completed Hickory Dickory Dock by Jim Aylesworth
Telling Time with Big Mama Cat by Dan Harper
What Time is it Mr. Crocodile? by Judy Sierra
Pigs on a Blanket by Amy Axelrod

Continents

Montessori: Map Work by Bobby George and June George
Counting the Continents by Ellen Mitten
National Geographic Kids Beginner's World Atlas by National Geographic
The ABCs of Continents by Bobbie Kalman

HISTORY

Sticks 'n Stones 'n Dinosaur Bones, by Ted Enik
I Feel Better with a Frog in My Throat, by Carlyn Beccia
Worst of Friends, by Suzanne Tripp Jurmain.
Pop! The Invention of Bubble Gum, by Meghan McCarthy
Sit-In, by Andrea Davis Pinkney
The World in Your Lunch Box, by Claire Emer
Noah Webster and His Words, by Jeri Chase Ferris
So, You Want to Be President, by Judith St. George

MAPS

Henri's Map by David Elias
Mapmaking with Children by David Sobel
A First Book o Mapping Skills: Follow that Map! By Scot Ritchie
Me on the Map by Joan Sweeney

SOUTH AMERICA

Looking for Something by Ann Nolan Clark

A Pen Pal for Max by Gloria Rand

We're Sailing to Galapagos by Lynne Cherry

The Littlest Llama by Jane Buxton

Up and down the Andes by Laurie Krebbs

Bibliburro by Jeannette Winter

The Chocolate Tree by Linda Lowery

Moon Rope by Lois Ehlert

CALENDAR

Snowy Flowy Blowy by Nancy Tafuri
Chicken Soup with Rice by Maurice Sendak
A Year of Beasts by Ashley Wolff
A Child's Calendar by John Updike, illustrated by Trina

Schart Hyman

Calendar by Myra Cohn Livingston, illustrated by Will Hillenbrand

A Year with Friends by John Seven, illustrated by Jana Christy

One Lighthouse, One Moon by Anita Lobel

How Do You Say It Today, Jesse Bear? by Nancy White Carlstrom, illustrated by Bruce Degen

Long Night Moon by Cynthia Rylant, illustrated by Mark Siegel

Around the Year by Tasha Tudor

LETTER WRITING

Can I Be Your Dog? by Troy Cummings

Dear Dragon: A Pen Pal Tale by Josh Funk, illustrated by Rodolfo Montalvo

Ten Thank-You Letters by Daniel Kirk

Dear Dinosaur by Chae Strathie, illustrated by Nicola O'Byrne

The Day the Crayons Quit by Drew Daywalt, illustrated by Oliver Jeffers

XO, OX: A Love Story by Adam Rex, illustrated by Scott Campbell

Dear Deer: A Book of Homophones by Gene Barretta

Dear Teacher by Amy Husband

I Wanna Iguana by Kren Kaufman Orloff, illustrated by David Catrow

The Jolly Postman by Allan Ahlberg, illustrated by Janet Ahlberg

A Letter to My Teacher by Deborah Hopkinson, illustrated by Nancy Carpenter

HANDWRITING/WRITING

Author: A True Story by Helen Lester

The Best Story by Eileen Spinelli, Illustrated by Anne Wilsdorf

My Book About Me by ME, Myself by Dr. Seuss

Rocket Writes a Story by Tad Hills

A Squiggly Story by Andrew Larsen and Mike Lowery

My Crayons Talk by Patricia Hubbard

The Crayon Box That Talked by Shane Derolf and Michael Letzig

Harold and the Purple Crayon by Crockett Johnson

Little Pencil Finds His Forever Friends by Christine Calabrese

Beautiful Oops! by Barney Saltzberg

The Line by Paula Bossio

A Line Can Be by Laura Ljungkvist

This is My Story by Rozanne Lanczak Williams

My Picture Story by Rozanne Lanczak Williams

Little Monster Becomes an Author by Rozanne Lanczak Williams

I Love to Write! by Rozanne Lanczak Williams

Little Plane Learns to Write by Stephen Savage

Write On, Carlos! by Stuart J. Murphy

FROGS

Frog on a Log by Kes Gray

The Icky Sticky Frog by Dawn Bentley

Leap, Frog, Leap! by Douglas Florian

Frog and Toad are Friends by Arnold Lobel

Growing Frogs: Read and Wonder by Vivian French

Hoppity Frog: A Slide and Seek Book by Emma Parrish

Freddy the Frogcaster by Janice Dean

Five Little Speckled Frogs by Nikki Smith

Frog and Fly by Jeff Mack

Jump, Frog, Jump! by Robert Kalan

Frogs by Gail Gibbons

Frogs and Toads and Tadpoles, Too! by Allan Fowler

A Frog's Life by Dona Rice

A Frog in the Bog by Karma Wilson
Frogs by Nic Bishop
Frog or Toad: How Do You Know? By Melissa Stewart
From Tadpole to Frog by Wendy Pfeffer
Frog by Susan Cooper

MONKEYS

Hug by Jez Alborough
Caps for Sale by Esphyr Slobodkina
Where's My Mon? by Julia Donaldson
In My Jungle by Sara Gillingham
Little Monkey Calms Down by Michael Dahl

NEIGHBORHOOD

A House Is a House for Me by Mary Ann Hoberman,
illustrated by Betty Fraser
Multicultural Fables & Fairytales by Tara McCarthy
How a House Is Built by Gail Gibbons
Exploring Our World: Neighborhoods & Communities by
Kathleen M. Hollenbeck
So Many Circles, So Many Squares by Tana Hoban
The Big Orange Splot by Daniel Pinkwater
In Lucia's Neighborhood by Pat Shewchuk and Marek
Colek
Look Where We Live! A First Book of Community Building
by Scot Ritchie.
In the Town All Year 'Round by Rotraut Suzanne Berner

SHADOWS

On a Dark, Dark Night by Jean Cochran, illustrated by
Jennifer Morris
Shadow Story by Nancy Willard, illustrated by David Diaz

Moonbear's Shadow by Frank Asch
Nothing Sticks like a Shadow by Ann Tompert
Papa Lucky's Shadow by Niki Daly
The Black Rabbit by Philippa Leathers
My Shadow by Robert Louis Stevenson, illustrations by Sara Sanches
Shadows by April Pulley Sayre
I Have a Friend by Keiko Narahashi
The Queen's Shadow by Cybele Young
Shadow Play by Bernie Zubrowski
Let the Shadows Speak by Franzeska G. Ewart
Shadows and Reflections by Tana Hoban
Shadows and Reflections by Daniel Nunn

GETTING TO KNOW YOU/STUDENT OF THE WEEK

The Pigeon Has to Go to School by Mo Willems
School's First Day of School by Adam Rex and Christian Robinson
Brown Bear Starts School by Sue Tarsky and Marina Aizen
Pirates Don't Go to Kindergarten! by Lisa Robinson and Eda Kaban
The King of Kindergarten by Derrick Barnes and Vanessa Brantley-Newton
The Day You Begin by Jacqueline Woodson
All Are Welcome by Alexandra Penfold
We Don't Eat Our Classmates by Ryan T. Higgins
You're Finally Here! by Melanie Watt
First Day Jitters by Julie Danneberg
The Name Jar by Yangsook Choi
The Exceptionally, Extraordinarily Ordinary First Day of School by Albert Lorenz The Book with No Pictures by B.J. Novak
How to Get Your Teacher Ready by Jean Reagan

Week 1:   **Monday**   **WINTER BREAK**

Winter Break – No School

No school – winter break

No school - winter break

No school – winter break

Winter break – no school

Week 1 Art Instructions

Winter break – no school

Reflection Journal

A journal is a vital part of the Montessori classroom. This is the space you will use to take notes about what is going well in the classroom and what needs to be tweaked for next week. As you commit to this practice every week, you will find that you have created a very useful diary that will help you learn and grow as a Montessori teacher.

"One test of the correctness of educational procedure is the happiness of the child."
— Maria Montessori

8:30am Circle: Read a book from the **HISTORY** selections. This can be the first day that you begin an "official" calendar time at circle time. Read my section on calendar time at the beginning of this guide.

History Bean Jar: Materials needed – a jar with a lid to hold the beans, a basket with dried large lima beans (or other variety). Lesson: Say, "I have something special to share with you today." Hold up the jar. Say, "This is an empty jar," Open the lid and place it on the tray. Hold the jar upside to indicate that it is empty. Place jar on the tray. Pick up the basket with beans and say, "This is a basket holding dried beans." Place the basket on the tray. Pick up a bean and say, "this is a bean." Take the bean and put it in the empty jar. Pick up the lid and put it on the jar. Hold up the jar and say, "I put one bean in our jar today. We are going to put one bean in our jar every day. Remember, History is the study about how people, places and things in our world have been recorded on our Earth. We are going to record every day by putting a bean in our jar." Every day at circle time, remember to have someone put a bean in the jar.

OPTION: YOU CAN INVITE CHILDREN TO KEEP TRACK OF TIME IN THIS WAY AT HOME.

Place the tray on the works shelf.

LESSONS – GIVEN IN THE GROUP OR INDIVIDUALLY:

THE WORLD MAP   **SOUTH AMERICA**
THREE PART CARDS

SOUTH AMERICA LIVING/NONLIVING

ART: Chalk Pastel Snake

11:30am Circle: Read a book from the **SOUTH AMERICA** selections. Introduce your materials from your Geography Album pertaining to South America. You may also purchase my kit on South America – CLICK HERE.

ABCS OF SOUTH AMERICA

A-Anaconda

B-Buenos Aires

2:30pm Circle: Read the book from the **CALENDAR** selections

SONG/MOVEMENT: Hello, hello, can you clap your hands?

Lyrics:

Hello, hello. Can you clap your hands? Hello, hello. Can you clap your hands? Can you stretch up high? Can you touch your toes? Can you turn around? Can you say, "Hello"? Hello, hello. Can you stamp your feet? Hello, hello. Can you stamp your feet? Can you stretch up high? Can you touch your toes? Can you turn around? Can you say, "Hello"? Hello, hello.

Can you clap your hands? Hello, hello. Can you stamp your feet?

Video: https://www.youtube.com/watch?v=fN1CyrOZK9M

SCIENCE: MELTING CHOCOLATE. Materials: small chocolate pieces of the same size (chocolate bar squares or chocolate chips), paper plate, pen and paper to record your results Demonstration: put one piece of chocolate on a paper plate and put it outside in the shade. Record how long it took for the chocolate to melt or if it wasn't hot enough to melt then record how soft it was after 10 minutes. Repeat the process but this time put the chocolate out in the sun. Record your results in the same way. Find other locations to test how long it takes for the chocolate to melt. Compare your results; in what conditions di the chocolate melt? If you have thermometers on hand, mark the temperature of the places that you placed the chocolate. line the glasses next to each other and fill them with different amounts of water. What's happening? At a certain temperature, your chocolate undergoes a physical change from a solid to a liquid (or somewhere in between. Other questions to ask? What can you do to reverse the process? What if you compared white chocolate and dark chocolate? What if you put a piece of aluminum foil between the paper plate and the chocolate?

<u>Chalk Pastel Snake:</u>

Materials:

Chalk pastels

Kleenex

Q-tips

Construction paper

Optional: hairspray

Steps:

1 -Choose ONE COLOR to outline the snake making a winding "S" shape.

2- Use other chalk colors to design your snake

3- use q-tips and Kleenex smudge and blend the chalk into a more nuanced design

4- to seal the chalk – spray with hairspray in a VERY VENTILATED PLACE AWAY FROM THE STUDENTS

8:30am Circle: Read a book from **HANDWRITING** selections. Begin to implement your handwriting practice becoming more intentional for your 2nd and 3rd year students. Read my section on handwriting at the beginning of this guide.

Yoga: choose two poses from the basket

GEOGRAPHY: Map your house. Talk about the parts of the house. You may offer some type of structure such as graph paper or copy paper or you may use popsicle sticks and glue and have the students adhere it to poster board or card board strips and then offer markers and crayons for them to draw the details of each of the areas inside their house.

11:30am Circle: Read a book from the **NEW YEAR** selections

COOKING: South American Vegetable and Rice Soup

This hearty soup blends the best of Caribbean soup ingredients – black beans, tomato, and rice – all in one. The rich tomato base wraps the vegetables, beans, and rice in herb-filled flavor.

Ingredients:
½ teaspoon extra-virgin olive oil
1 onion, roughly chopped
4 garlic cloves, minced
1 teaspoon oregano
¼ teaspoon ground allspice
½ teaspoon ground cumin
4 cups low-sodium vegetable stock
4 fresh husked tomatillos (can substitute green or red tomatoes)

1 (14.5 oz.) can diced tomatoes
1 cup canned black beans, drained and rinsed
½ cup frozen corn kernels
1 medium green zucchini or yellow squash, halved and then sliced in halfmoons
½ teaspoon chipotle or cayenne pepper
¼ teaspoon salt
1 cup cooked brown rice
2 tablespoons fresh cilantro (optional garnish)

Instructions

1. Heat the oil in a large saucepan over medium high heat and cook the onion until it becomes translucent, about 2 minutes.

2. Toss in the garlic, oregano, allspice and cumin, and cook for another 2 minutes, stirring so the garlic doesn't brown.

3. Pour in the vegetable stock, the tomatillos and can of tomatoes. Bring to boil, turn the heat down, and allow it to simmer for 10 minutes.

4. Add the beans, corn, squash, chipotle sauce, and salt. Bring back to a boil, turn down the heat, and simmer for 5 minutes.

5. Add the cup of cooked brown rice (newly cooked or from leftovers) into the soup for the last 4-5 minutes of cook-time.

This recipe makes 6 servings

2:30pm Circle: Read a book from the **SOUTH AMERICA** selections.

ABCs of South America:

C-Capybara

D- Dulce de Leche

LESSONS:

Teens Board Review
Hundred Board/Hundred Chain Review

8:30am Circle: Read a book from the **HISTORY** selections

HISTORY: STATUE. Materials needed: a small statue of a child. If you do not have this available, you can still teach it with music and/or a stopwatch. Presentation: Say, "This is a statue. It is a representation of a child. It looks like a child. Can this statue move on its own?" Discuss. Say, "Today we are going to play a game called Statues." Place the statue in the middle of the circle. Invite the students to stand up and move slowly around the circle. This is where you can incorporate music. You can either give the instruction that when the music stops, the children need to hold as still as a statue, or you can have them follow that direction when the music stops. Next have them watch the clock or use the stopwatch and stop it when they come out of the statue position. Say, "whether we are moving or standing as still as a statue, time goes by. Keeping track of time is a part of history,"

YOGA: choose 2 poses from the basket

ART: Life cycle of a Frog. MATERIALS: green paint, black crayon, white, green, yellow playdoh.

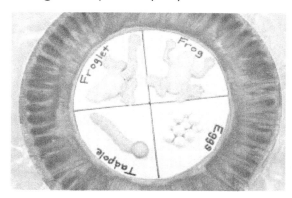

Life Cycle of a Frog

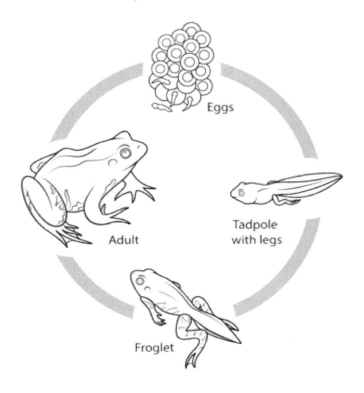

Eggs

Tadpole
with legs

Adult

Froglet

LESSONS:

**PARTS OF A FROG
WORK**

FROG MATCHING

LIFE CYCLE OF A FROG

11:30am Circle: read a book from the **CONTINENT** selections. Introduce the idea of creating projects at home that represent South America (see notes at the beginning of the guide on how to create an extension of learning in Geography).

ABCS OF SOUTH AMERICA:

E-EMPANADAS
F- FROGS

SCIENCE: Baking soda and Vinegar Chemical Reaction. MATERIALS: baking soda, vinegar, a container big enough to hold everything, paper towels or a cloth. INSTRUCTIONS: place some baking soda into your container. Pour in your vinegar, watch as the reaction takes place. What's Happening? The baking soda is a base while the vinegar is an acid. When they react together they form carbonic acid which is very unstable. It instantly breaks apart into water and carbon dioxide, which creates all the fizzing as it escapes the solutions.

OPTION: This can transition nicely into making a volcano since we discussed a volcano in our North America section last month.

2:30pm Circle: Read a book from the **FROG** selections

LESSONS:

Presentations of Base Ten – Decimal System Symbol (Review)

SIGHT WORDS INTRODUCTION AND REVIEW: THE, OF, AND, A, TO

SONG/MOVEMENT:

Five little speckled frogs
Sat on a speckled log
Eating some most delicious bugs.
YUM! YUM!
One jumped into the pool,
Where it was nice and cool,

Now there are four green speckled frogs!
GLUB! GLUB!

Four little speckled frogs
Sat on a speckled log
Eating some most delicious bugs.
YUM! YUM!
One jumped into the pool,
Where it was nice and cool,
Now there are three green speckled frogs!
GLUB! GLUB!

Three little speckled frogs
Sat on a speckled log
Eating some most delicious bugs.
YUM! YUM!
One jumped into the pool,
Where it was nice and cool,
Now there are two green speckled frogs!
GLUB! GLUB!

Two little speckled frogs
Sat on a speckled log
Eating some most delicious bugs.
YUM! YUM!
One jumped into the pool,
Where it was nice and cool,
Now there is one green speckled frog!
GLUB! GLUB!

One little speckled frog
Sat on a speckled log
Eating some most delicious bugs.
YUM! YUM!
He jumped into the pool,

Where it was nice and cool,
Now there are no green speckled frogs!

8:30am Circle: Read a story from the **NEIGHBORHOOD** selections

GEOGRAPHY/ART: HOME OF Buenos Aires

Discuss what is similar about homes in our neighborhood in our Country and homes in Buenos Aires – show pictures of the homes in your neighborhood and show the pictures of Buenos Aires in this guide.

OPTIONAL: INVITE THE STUDENTS TO MAKE A MAP OF THEIR NEIGHBORHOOD

ART: Create a Neighborhood you might see in Buenos Aires using **Metal Insets or Geometric Cabinet.** Use Construction paper to colorful results. You will also need: glue, scissors, easel paper.

YOGA: Pick a few cards from the yoga basket

Cooking/Food Tasting: Plantain Chips (or a family can fry plantains and bring them to share)

LESSONS:

Neighborhoods Around the World Nomenclature Cards

South American Pin Poking of the map (Big Work)

11:30am Circle- Read a book from the **SOUTH AMERICA** selections.

G- Guanaco
H-Howler monkey

2:30pm Circle: Read a Book from the **NEW YEAR** selections

LESSONS:

Cities in your State Tracing Cards

Homes of Buenos Aires

8:30am Circle: Read a book from the **SHADOWS** selections

HISTORY: SHADOW DRAWING. Materials: sunny day, sidewalk, basket of chalk. Say, "Many years ago, the first people on our Earth would tell the time by watching the sun. It is important never to stare at the sun. But do you see where the sun is this morning?" Next, say," The sun is in the sky and we are going to see how time travels by watching the sun move. We can do this by shadow drawing." You will be tracing the children's bodies o the sidewalks. Next say, "we are all going inside to continue our activities. IN one hour (or some designated time), we will go outside again and see where the sun has traveled. "The children will then find their chalk drawn shape and see if the shadow is in the same place. You can continue this exercise by drawing a second shadow and again observe the movement. At the end of the exercise, say" today we watched time move by drawing around someone's shadow during different times of day. Keeping track of time is a part of history."

LESSONS:

Adjectives Game (review)

Presentation on golden beads – Addition (review)

Presentation on golden beads -Subtraction (review)

ART: Exploring Light with Shadow puppets:

Exploring Light with DIY Shadow Puppets

- Cardboard (or a heavier card stock paper)

- Kebab Skewers or wooden dowels

- Black Paint

- Scissors

- Tape (packaging or duct tape work best)

Trace/sketch the puppet you want to make on cardboard. Then cut out and paint. Tape the skewers to the back once dry.

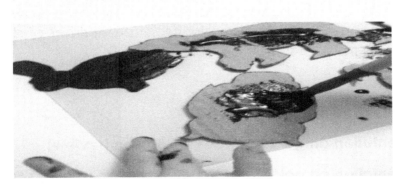

11:30 Circle: Read a story from the **CALENDAR** selections

SONG/MOVEMENT: Hello!

Lyrics: Hello! Hello! Hello, how are you? (Repeat) I'm good! I'm great! I'm wonderful! (Repeat) Hello! Hello! Hello, how are

you? (Repeat) I'm tired. I'm hungry. I'm not so good. (Repeat)
Hello! Hello! Hello, how are you? (Repeat 3x)

Video: https://www.youtube.com/watch?v=tVlcKp3bWH8

YOGA: choose two poses from the basket

2:30pm Circle: Read a book from the **CONTINENT**
selections

ABCs of North America

I-Iguazu Falls
J-Jabuticaba
Review all the things we have learned about South
America. Talk about the places the children would like
to travel to see and all the places they have gone. Make
a brainstorming map for the exercise and date it and
add it to your classroom environment.

LESSONS:

Famous Landmarks in our State three-part cards

Week 2 Art Instructions

Chalk Pastel Snake: Materials: Chalk pastels, Kleenex, Q-tips, construction paper, Optional: hairspray. Instructions: Choose ONE COLOR to outline the snake making a winding "S" shape. Use other chalk colors to design your snake. Use q-tips and Kleenex smudge and blend the chalk into a more nuanced design. To seal the chalk – spray with hairspray in a VERY VENTILATED PLACE AWAY FROM THE STUDENTS

Life cycle of a Frog: Materials: green paint, black crayon, white, green, yellow playdoh. This is an opportunity for the students to make playdoh.

Exploring Light with DIY Shadow Puppets: Cardboard (or a heavier card stock paper), Kebab Skewers or wooden dowels, Black Paint, Scissors, Tape (packaging or duct tape work best). Instructions: Trace/sketch the puppet you want to make on cardboard, then cut out and paint. Attach skewers with duct tape.

Reflection Journal

Maria Montessori combined knowledge, observation and common sense to create an environment that would feed the minds and sprits of the children. This is your charge as a Montessori guide.

8:30 am Circle: Read a book from the **CALENDARS** Selections.

HISTORY: Review the parts of a calendar. Say, "this is a calendar. There are many types of calendars. All calendars help us record time and experience history." Pass the calendar around the circle so that everyone can take a close look at it. If possible, on different days throughout the month, show a linear calendar, a magnetic calendar, a pocket calendar, an advent calendar.

LESSONS:

Noun/Verb Connections Game (Review)

EXPERIMENT: Cut Ice Cubes in Half Like Magic. Materials: one ice cube, a piece of fishing line with a weight tied to each end, a container, a tray. INSTRUCTIONS: turn the container upside down and put it on a tray. Place the ice cube on top of the upside-down container. Rest the fishing line over the ice cube so that the weights are left dangling over the sides of the container. Watch it for around 5 minutes. What's happening? The pressure from the two weights pull the string through the ice cube by melting the ice directly under the fishing line. This is like ice skating where the blades of a skater melt directly underneath, allowing the skater to move smoothly on a thin layer of water.

ART: paper plate parrot

paper plate
PARROT

11:30am Circle: Read a book from **SOUTH AMERICA** selections – allow for any presentations made at home.

ABCs of South America

K-Kakao
L- Los llanos

YOGA: Choose two poses from the basket

2:30pm Circle: Read a book from the **SHADOW** selections.

LESSONS:

Presentations on Golden Beads – Multiplication

8:30am Circle: Read a book from the **NEIGHBORHOODS** selections

Talk about the places we go to in our neighborhood. Talk about HOW we get to those places/what kind of transportation we can use. Talk about HOW we know where to go.

YOGA: Choose two poses from the basket

GEOGRAPHY: DIRECTIONALITY – WHERE IS NORTH. Materials: Compass, label for NORTH WITH AN ARROW – HERE IS A SMAPLE BELOW. Say, "a compass is a very useful tool. Tools help us to do things. A compass helps us to find directions. A compass has a needle that always points to the north." Take out the compass. Say, "My compass has a needle that points to the north. I need to hold my compass very flat and still. If I do, it will point to the north." Have some of the children try. This can be left on the shelf and on another day, you can offer a lesson where you discover which wall in your room is the north wall.

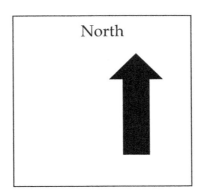

LESSONS:

SEQUENCING CARDS (review)

WHICH ONE IS DIFFERENT SORTING CARDS (review)

ART: Ojo de Rios

How to Make Ojo de Dios

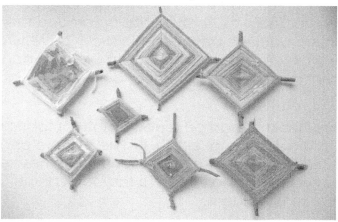

Materials: 2 sticks or twigs roughly the same length. In a pinch, you can use Popsicle sticks. Something to weave onto the sticks. Some examples are:

- Scrap yarn

- Fabric torn into strips measuring about 1/2" wide and knotted together end to end

- Safety twine from the hardware store.

- Leather lacing

- Para cord or thin rope

Optional materials: sequins, beads, or contrasting scrap yarn and yarn needle

Instructions: Cross the 2 sticks at their center points and wrap the yarn around the center and tie a square knot. This doesn't need to be a tight or pretty knot; you're just anchoring the yarn around the sticks. You will wrap the yarn around the Ojo in a clockwise direction. Starting at the 3 o'clock stick, then going to the 6 o-clock stick, then 9 o-clock, and so on.

Wrap the yarn around each individual stick by bringing the yarn over the stick, then wrapping around the back and coming back up between the stick you're wrapping and the stick you just wrapped. Bring the yarn back over the current stick, and onward to the next stick, and repeat.

When you need to add on a new length of fabric or thread to the wrapping length, just tie the two ends together with a square knot. I never mind if these ends show, but you can coax them to the back of the Ojo if you prefer to hide them.

When finished with your weaving, just tie the end around one of the sticks.

Additional ideas

Sew accent stripes right onto the woven area. Use a yarn needle to sew between the strands of yarn in a contrast color. Loosely tie this yarn off on the back with a knot.

11:30am Circle: Read a book from the **FROG** selections.

COOKING: Papaya-Mango Smoothie

Christopher Columbus referred to the papaya as "the fruit of angels" and that's not a stretch! One cup of the sunset-hued fruit—native to Mexico and South America—packs healthy doses of vitamin C, folate, and beta-carotene. Give your kids a taste of the tropics by blending 1 cup each of sliced papaya and mango, 8 oz of coconut water, ½ cup of kefir and a tablespoon of honey into a nutrition-packed smoothie.

2:30pm Circle- Read a book from the **South AMERICA** selections

ABCs of South America

M- Mount Fitz Roy
N- Nisperos

Week 3   Wednesday   STUDENT OF THE WEEK

8:30am Circle: Read a book from the **STUDENT OF THE WEEK/GETTING TO KNOW YOU selections.** young children love to be in the spotlight and having a "Star of the week" is a great way to honor each individual student.

The star of the week concept is meant for students to share a little bit about themselves with their classmates. By taking center stage, students feel a sense of pride while they get to share fascinating facts and stories about themselves and their life with their peers. It also helps to build a sense of community because students are celebrating each other every week. Say, "On Friday one of you will get an envelope in your backpack that lets your parents know you are student of the week. You will answer questions, gather pictures and create a collage to share in class with your friends."

GEOGRAPHY: DIRECTIONALITY – FINDING NORTH, SOUTH, EAST, WEST –

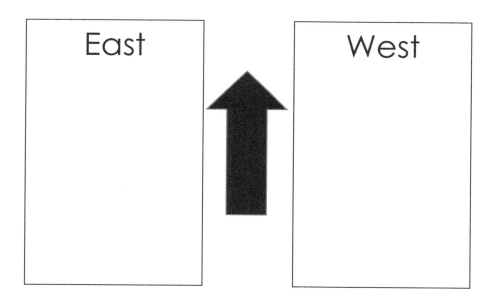

LESSONS:

Presentation of Golden Beads – Division

SIGHT WORDS: AS, WITH, THEY, I, HIS

11:30am Circle:

SONG/MOVEMENT: Bread and Butter: Welcome and Goodbye Song

Lyrics: Bread and butter Marmalade and Jam Let's say hello as quiet as we can (whisper: hello) ...loud as we can ...slow as we can ...fast as we can ...high as we can ...low as we can ...nice as we can

Video: https://www.youtube.com/watch?v=Tx61o23Vvns

YOGA: Choose a few cards from the basket

2:30pm Circle: Read a book from the **SOUTH AMERICA** selections

ABCs of South America

O-Ocelot
P- Perito Moreno Glacier

Pull out the south America Puzzle Map and review the countries on the map.

Week 3   **Thursday**   **GETTING TO KNOW YOU**

8:30am Circle: Read a book from the **GETTING TO KNOW YOU** selections

Cooking/food tasting: *dulce de leche COOKIES*

LESSONS:

PARTS OF A MONKEY NOMENCLATURE Cards

LIFE CYCLE OF A MONKEY

QUESTIONS GAMES

EXPERIMENT: What Absorbs more heat? Materials: 2 identical drinking glasses or jars, water, thermometer, 2 elastic bands, white paper, black paper. Instructions: wrap the white paper around one of the glasses using an elastic band. Do the same with the black paper and he other glass. Fill the glasses with the exact same amount of water. Leave the glasses out in the sun for a couple of hours before returning to measure the temperature of the water in each. What's happening? Dark surfaces such as the black paper absorb more light and heat than the lighter ones such as the white paper. After measuring the temperatures of the water, the glass with the black paper around it should be hotter than the other. Lighter surfaces reflect more light.

11:30AM Circle: Read a book from the **South America** selections.

ABCs OF South America

Q-Quinoa
R- Rumba

SONG/MOVEMENT: Find music that one would dance the rumba to and invite the children to move to the beat.

2:30pm Circle: Read a book from the **Monkey** selections.

LESSONS:

Things that tell time 3-part cards (review)

0'clock and :30 time on the clock 3-part cards

Have students bring in their plants that they grew over Winter break along with the charts they created.

8:30am Circle Read a book from the **GETTING TO KNOW YOU** selections. Set up your expectations for how you will incorporate Student of the Week in the classroom.

YOGA: pick one or two poses from the basket

ART: Lunch bag Monkey puppet

Supplies: paper lunch bags, Card or cover stock, glue sticks, Elmer's glue, googly eyes, crayons.

Instructions: Make a template shown above and make copies. Color the parts before cutting the pieces out. Using Elmer's glue, attach the head to the foldout part of the paper bag. Glue on the face piece with eyes and then the part with the mouth partially covering it. Glue the arms in between the fold of each side of the bag. Attach the hands to the arms. Glue the tail sticking out of the fold. If you prefer googly eyes, glue them on last.

11:30am Circle:

COOKING: Quick and Easy Corn Fritters

Ingredients

- 3 cups corn kernels (See Kelly's Note)
- 1 cup all-purpose flour
- 1 Tablespoon sugar
- 1 teaspoon baking powder

- 2 large eggs, lightly beaten

- 3/4 cup heavy cream

- Vegetable oil, for frying

- Sliced scallions, for serving

- Sour cream or garlic aioli, for serving

Instructions

In a large bowl, stir together the corn kernels, flour, sugar, baking powder, 1/2 teaspoon salt and 1/4 teaspoon pepper.

Stir in the eggs and heavy cream until the batter is well-combined.

Line a plate with paper towels. Coat the bottom of a large sauté pan with vegetable oil and place it over medium-high heat. Once the oil is hot, scoop 2- to 3-tablespoon mounds of the corn batter into the pan, spreading it lightly into a flat, circular shape. Cook the fritters for 2 to 3 minutes, then flip them once and cook them an additional 3 minutes until they're golden brown and cooked through. Transfer the fritters to the paper towel-lined plate, season them immediately with salt and repeat the cooking process with the remaining batter, adding more oil to the pan as needed.

Garnish the corn fritters with scallions and serve them with sour cream or garlic aioli for dipping.

Makes about 15 fritters

Note:

Fresh or frozen (thawed) corn kernels will work in this recipe. If you use frozen corn, drain off any excess liquid after it thaws.

SONG/MOVEMENT: FOLLOW MONKEY

Instructions: The children form a circle and one child, (the monkey) goes to the middle and makes up a dance or movement for everyone else to imitate, then takes a bow and moves to the outside. All the children get a chance to be the monkey separately. At the end of the song all the children step in the middle to do all the new movements initiated by all the monkeys.

Lyrics: Monkey see, monkey do. Do you want to follow monkey too? There's a monkey in the middle, just because you got to do what that little monkey does. Follow monkey, follow monkey, follow monkey, follow monkey. Chorus: Now the monkey in the middle takes a bow, there's a new little monkey gonna show us how. Monkey's in the middle, just because, you got to do what that little monkey does. Follow monkey, follow monkey, follow monkey, follow monkey. Repeat chorus (3x) Monkey see, monkey do. Step in the middle, be a monkey too. We're all monkeys in the middle, just because we can do anything any monkey does. Follow monkey, follow monkey, follow monkey, follow monkey.

VIDEO: https://www.youtube.com/watch?v=ZGxvCTCWWhM

2:30pm Circle: Read a book from the **SOUTH AMERICA** selections

ABCs of SOUTH AMERICA

S- Salar de Uyuni
T-Tapir

Week 3 Art Instructions

<u>Paper plate parrot: Materials-</u> paper plate, scissors, large googly eyes, glue, markers, construction paper, tissue paper. INSTRUCTIONS: cut paper plate down the middle. Decorate one half by drawing a line down the middle and coloring with two marker colors. Glue tissue paper onto the second half of the paper plate. Cut a piece of construction paper into long strips. Glue all the pieces together and add the googly eye.

<u>Ojo de Dios</u>: **Materials:** 2 sticks or twigs roughly the same length. In a pinch, you can use Popsicle sticks. Something to weave onto the sticks. Some examples are: Scrap yarn, Fabric torn into strips measuring about 1/2" wide and knotted together end to end, Safety twine from the hardware store, Leather lacing, Para cord or thin rope. Optional materials: sequins, beads, or contrasting scrap yarn and yarn needle. **Instructions:** Cross the 2 sticks at their center points and wrap the yarn around the center and tie a square knot. This doesn't need to be a tight or pretty knot; you're just anchoring the yarn around the sticks. You will wrap the yarn around the Ojo in a clockwise direction. Starting at the 3 o'clock stick, then going to the 6 o-clock stick, then 9 o-clock, and so on. Wrap the yarn around each individual stick by bringing the yarn over the stick, then wrapping around the back and coming back up between the stick you're wrapping and the stick you just wrapped. Bring the yarn back over the current stick, and onward to the next stick, and repeat. When you need to add on a new length of fabric or thread to the wrapping length, just tie the two ends together with a square knot. I never mind if these ends show, but you can coax them to the back of the Ojo if you prefer to hide them. When finished with your weaving, just tie the end around one of the sticks.

<u>Paper bag Monkey puppet</u>: **Supplies:** paper lunch bags, Card or cover stock, glue sticks, Elmer's glue, googly eyes, crayons. **Instructions:** Make a template shown above and make copies. Color the parts before cutting the pieces out. Using Elmer's glue, attach the head to the foldout part of the paper bag. Glue on the face piece with eyes and then the part with the mouth partially covering it. Glue the arms in between the fold of each side of the bag. Attach the hands to the arms. Glue the tail sticking out of the fold. If you prefer googly eyes, glue them on last.

Reflection Journal

What activities did the children really connect with this week? What do you notice about the environment of your classroom? What area of the room did the children experience the most self-motivation? How can you bring that into other areas of the room?

8:30am Circle: This is the first "Star Student of the Week." Decide how you would like to incorporate it into your calendar time.

LESSONS

Lunar new year nomenclature cards

Parts of a letter three-part cards

ART: Chinese Lanterns.

Materials needed:

- One sheet **red paper**
- Two to three sheets **gold paper**
- Pencil and ruler
- Regular Scissors
- Scissors with fun shape (optional)
- Glue
- Tape
- Stapler
- Use the pencil and ruler to trace lines about 3/4" apart perpendicular and along the whole length of the red paper

- Use the scissors to cut through the lines leaving approximately 1/2" at the top uncut
- This will form the bars that will form the balloon of the lantern.

- Use some tape to hold the bottom of the bars together

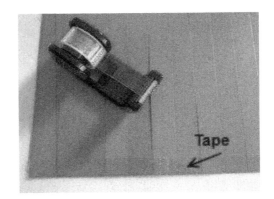

Using the fun-shape scissor, or the regular scissors if you don't have one, cut thin strips of gold paper

- Glue the trimmings to the lantern bars

- Fold 1/2" at the top and bottom of the red paper

- You can use the ruler and scissors to make a light crease, so it folds easily

- Roll the red paper into a cylinder. You can secure it with a couple of staples just to make sure it won't come off, the other side stays loose

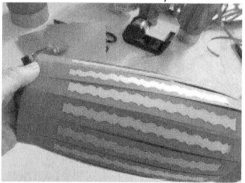

- Cut two stripes of gold paper 1/2" thick

- Glue them to the top and bottom of the lantern (it covers all the tape, staples, etc.)

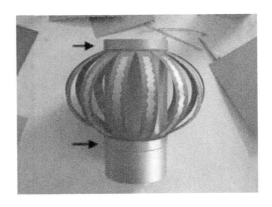

- Make the handle with a strip of gold paper. Glue on both sides at the top.

YOGA: choose two poses from the basket

11:30am Circle:

Story Time: Read a book from the **LUNAR NEW YEAR** selections.

LESSONS:

STAMP GAME PRESENTATION

2:30pm Circle: Read a book from the **MONKEYS** selections

Week 4　　　　　　**Tuesday**　　　　　　**LUNAR NEW YEAR**

8:30am Circle: Read a book from the **LUNAR NEW YEAR** selections.

Lessons:

SQUARING CHAINS (1-10) (REVIEW)

LETTER WRITING WORK

SIGHT WORDS: BUT, ALL, NOT, WHAT, WERE

Yoga: choose two poses from the basket

11:30am Circle: Read a book from the **LETTER WRITING** selections

Experiment: DISSOLVING Sugar at Higher Heats

Materials needed: sugar cubes, cold water in a clear glass, hot water in a clear glass, spoon for stirring. INSTRUCTIONS: make sure the glasses have equal amount of water. Put a sugar cube in the cold water and stir with the spoon until the sugar disappears. Repeat this process until the sugar stops dissolving – keep track of how many cubes you added. This means the sugar is gathering on the bottom rather than dissolving. Repeat the same process in the hot water. What's happening? Another name for the liquids inside the glass is solution. When the solution can no longer dissolve the sugar, it becomes a saturated solution, this means that sugar starts forming on the bottom of the cup. Why does the hot water dissolve more? Faster moving molecules which are spread farther apart than the molecules in the cold water.

2:30pm Circle: Read a Book from the **Handwriting** selections

Week 4 | **Wednesday** | **Letter Writing**

8:30am Circle: Remember to incorporate Star Student, any projects that have come in from South America work at home with Calendar time.

YOGA: choose 2 poses from the basket

SONG/MOVEMENT: Five Little Monkeys

Five little monkeys jumping on the bed. One fell off and bumped his head. Mama called the doctor and the doctor said, "No more monkeys jumping on the bed!" Four little monkeys jumping on the bed. One fell off and bumped his head. Mama called the doctor and the doctor said, "No more monkeys jumping on the bed!" Three little monkeys jumping on the bed. One fell off and bumped her head. Mama called the doctor and the doctor said, "No more monkeys jumping on the bed!" Two little monkeys jumping on the bed. One fell off and bumped his head. Mama called the doctor and the doctor said, "No more monkeys jumping on the bed!" One little monkey jumping on the bed. She fell off and bumped her head. Mama called the doctor and the doctor said, "No more monkeys jumping on the bed!"

LESSONS:

Cubing Chains (1-10) Review

PIN POKING SOUTH AMERICA MAP (CONTINUED)

PRESENTATION ON STAMP GAME: ADDITION

ART: South American Amate Bark Painting

What you'll need:

– 6 x 9" brown or tan paper (paper bags or craft paper works well as does construction paper)

– Tempera paints in red, white, yellow, green and blue (to make regular tempera paint stand out against the brown paper, add a bit of white to the green, yellow and blue. It'll brighten it just enough)

– Black "Sharpie" marker

Tear the edges off a piece of colored construction paper. Use thumb and pointer fingers on both hands and *slowly* tear. If you don't have colored construction paper, use craft paper or even paper bags.

Find images on the Internet representing Mexican Folk Art. Have the kids draw a border around the paper then added fanciful birds, Mexican suns and flowers to the middle

After the drawing is done, it's time to paint.

Add decorative border with a pen or sharpie

south

11:30am Circle:

Story Time: Read a book from the **TIME** selections.

2:30pm Circle: Read a book from MAP selections

ABCs of South America

U-URUGUAY
V-VENEZUALA

Week 4   **Thursday**   **SOUTH AMERICA REVIEW**

8:30am Circle: Read one of the books from the **SOUTH AMERICA** selections

Say, "Let's review what symbols we have learned that represent South America" and then go through the ones you have talked about up this point.

LESSONS:

SOUTH AMERICA GEOGRAPHY FOLDER (review)

SOUTH AMERICA PLANT/ANIMAL SORTING CARDS (review)

WHAT NUMBER COMES BEFORE____? AFTER? (review)

COMPOUND WORDS (review)

GEOGRAPHY: Make a treasure map
Materials: Easel paper, colored pencils, box with a lid, a small item, an envelope to place the item in.

(NOTE: THIS IS SOMETHING THAT WILL BE A POPULAR ITEM ON YOUR ART SHELF. AFTER THE BARK PAINTING PROJECT, I WOULD HAVE EXTRA PIECES OF LARGE BROWN PAPER BAGS THAT ARE CUT TO CONFORM WITH THE BARK PAINTING WORK OR THE TREASURE MAP WORK.)

For this lesson, we are going to confine the map area to an area in the room or at the school like the playground. The child will map a simple map of the area with the major items found in the area. For example, the practical life map would have the shelve, the snack table, the food preparation table, etc. On another day, have a child take the "treasure" and hide it in the area you have mapped. Say, "this is a map of the practical life area. Gather around me because today we are going on a treasure hunt." Make sure begin you begin that you have added arrows to YOUR map to indicate the direction you need to go to find the treasure. Discuss which way we need to go in order to follow the arrows shown on the map. Talk about what the "X" means on your map. Once you find the treasure, say "we have found the treasure! We used a map today to find a treasure. Maps are very important to help us find our way in the world. You can also incorporate your direction signs in the room throughout this lesson.

11:30am Circle:

YOGA: choose 2 poses from the basket

Story Time Read a book from the **TIME** Selections

2:30pm Circle:

Play 1-minute Silence Game or ask the children to close their eyes and listen to some peaceful music for one minute. Talk about what changes happen in Winter.

Week 4　　　　　**Friday**　　　　**LAND WATER AIR REVIEW**

8:30 Circle: Read a story from the **TU BU SHEVAT** selections

YOGA: choose two poses from the basket

LESSONS:

LAND WATER AIR NOMENCLATURE CARDS (REVIEW)

Opposites matching work (review)

Sequencing Cards (review)

11:30am Circle: Read a story from the **GETTING TO KNOW YOU** Selections. A FINAL CONVERSATION WITH THIS WEEK'S STAR STUDENT.

EXPERIMENT: Make an egg Float in Saltwater

Materials: one egg, water, salt, a tall drinking glass

Instructions: pour water into the glass until the glass is about half full. Stir in lots of salt (about 6 tablespoons). Carefully pour in plain water until it is NEARLY FULL- do NOT mix the salty water with the plain water. Gently lower the egg into the water and watch what happens. What's happening? Sale water is denser than ordinary tap water. The denser the liquid the easier it is for an object to float in it. When you lower the egg into the liquid it drops through the normal tap water until is reaches the salty water, at this point the eater is dense enough for the egg to float.

2:30pm Circle: Read a book from the **SOUTH AMERICA** selections.

ABCs of SOUTH America:

　　　　W- WOLF　　　　X- XRAY TETRA

Week 4 Art Instructions

Chinese Lanterns: Materials needed: One sheet red paper, Two to three sheets gold paper, Pencil and ruler, regular Scissors, Scissors with fun shape (optional), Glue, tape, Stapler. INSTRUCTIONS: Use the pencil and ruler to trace lines about 3/4" apart perpendicular and along the whole length of the red paper. Use the scissors to cut through the lines leaving approximately 1/2" at the top uncut. This will form the bars that will form the balloon of the lantern. Use some tape to hold the bottom of the bars together. Using the fun-shape scissor, or the regular scissors if you don't have one, cut thin strips of gold paper. Glue the trimmings to the lantern bars. Fold 1/2" at the top and bottom of the red paper. You can use the ruler and scissors to make a light crease, so it folds easily. Roll the red paper into a cylinder. You can secure it with a couple of staples just to make sure it won't come off; the other side stays loose. Cut two stripes of gold paper 1/2" thick. Glue them to the top and bottom of the lantern (it covers all the tape, staples, etc.) Make the handle with a strip of gold paper. Glue on both sides at the top.

South American Amate Bark Painting: MATERIALS: 6 x 9" brown or tan paper (paper bags or craft paper works well as does construction paper, Tempera paints in red, white, yellow, green and blue (to make regular tempera paint stand out against the brown paper, add a bit of white to the green, yellow and blue. It'll brighten it just enough), Black "Sharpie" marker. Instructions: Tear the edges off a piece of colored construction paper. Use thumb and pointer fingers on both hands and *slowly* tear. If you don't have colored construction paper, use craft paper or even paper bags. Find images on the Internet representing Mexican Folk Art. Have the kids draw a border around the paper then added fanciful birds, Mexican suns and flowers to the middle. After the drawing is done, it's time to paint. Add decorative border with a pen or sharpie.

Reflection Journal

Which works stimulated the joy of learning in the children. What other related activity could be integrated into the plans?

General Instructions

Missing or Broken Pieces

It is important that if any work is missing a piece it is removed from the work shelf until the missing piece are found or replaced. Keep labeled containers of extra pieces in a supply cabinet. The child receives a demonstration, in Montessori language we call this a lesson, before doing a work. Lessons are given without unnecessary talking. Do each step slowly- even more slowly that you can imagine- and deliberately exaggerated movements. This draws the child's attention to your what your hands are doing.

Water work

Make fill lines on the inside of the bowls and pitchers with a permanent marker for control of error for filling various water works. Put on a waterproof apron at the beginning of a water lesson.

Art Lessons

Put on an apron or smock at the beginning of an art lesson if it uses glue or paint. Keep newspaper available for placing under work. Once the easel painting lesson is given, the easel is always available in the classroom.

The Three Period Lesson

The three-period lesson is done when working one on one with a child and is used to introduce new terms or names of things.

Examples of phrasings-

1. "This is a ..."
2. "Show me the ..."

3. Give me the ..."
4. What is this?

Generic Work

Pattern Blocks-wooden or plastic pieces in various geometric shapes.

Puzzle- Look for puzzles with a knob. The knob helps to develop the muscles for holding a pencil. This lesson is given using no words.

Ideas for Lesson Extensions in Each

Area of the Classroom

Practical Life Work (and some extensions)

Tongs Sponge Tower – 10 foam sponges of various colors cut in half, tongs. Lesson – using tongs, carefully stack the sponges one on top of the other. When all 10 ae carefully placed.

Paring Socks- this is a basket of children's socks. You can pair them and turn the cuffs.

Parts of the Paintbrush- you can make three-part cards, or you can trace a paintbrush, print the words that are the parts of the paintbrush: handle, ferrule, hairs, tip. Laminate. Have a real paintbrush available as part of the work.

Right and Left shoes- create different shoes – left and right – and laminate it and make is available on the shelf as a pairing/matching work.

Another option: have all the children take off their shoes and put them in the center of the circle. Go around the circle and let a child pick a shoe that is not her own. Find the pair and then place the pair of shoes in front of the child she thinks they belong to.

Sensorial

Color Swatch Matching: Pairs of color swatches from a paint store

Lesson: Put swatches in a pile. Take the top swatch card and put it on the left side of the workspace. Take another card and put it next to the card – is it the same or different color? If yes, place it next to its partner. If no, put it on the right side of the workspace. Continue until all the swatches are matched.

Calendar and Math Work

Calendar Tiles: Age 3+

Purchase 31 one-inch white ceramic tiles. With a permanent marker print the number 1-31. ON paper, make a blank calendar with one-inch squares and laminate.

Lesson-Place the blank calendar on the left. Place the numbered calendar next to it. Have your tiles available. Look at the calendar and place the numbers in the appropriate on the blank calendar using the numbered calendar as your guide.

Calendar Tracing Age 3+

On One copy of the blank calendar as described above, fill in the numerals for the current month and laminate it.

Lesson- Place paper on the calendar and trace the numerals.

Leaf Stair-Press leaves in a leaf press (if available) and then laminate. Number cards 1-5 or 1-10, felt square

Lesson-Place the number cards vertically down the left side pf the felt. Point to and say "1" and place a leaf to the right of the numeral 1. Point to 2 and say "2" and place two leaves to the right. Continue until all the leaves are placed. The control of error is having the exact amount of leaves for the child to place.

Language Work

Preparation for Writing

Practical Life and Sensorial exercises that develop muscles of the fingers and eye/hand and fine motor control- work that involves picking up kernels of popcorn, grasping knobbed puzzles and the knobbed cylinders. It continues with tracing work, insets and sandpaper letters.

Preparation for Reading

Reading begins with silence, listening, sequencing, patterning, naming objects and shapes, matching and classification of objects. It continues with the sandpaper letters and moveable alphabet.

The Silence Game

The Importance of the Silence Game

"One day I had the idea of using silence to test the children's keenness of hearing, so I thought of calling them by name, in a low whisper.... This exercise in patient waiting demanded a patience that I thought impossible."
—Maria Montessori, *The Secret of Childhood*

To Montessori's surprise, when she experimented with this very first Silence Game, the group of over 40 children waited quietly and patiently to hear their names whispered. After they refused the sweets, she thought they might need as a reward, Montessori reflected, "They seemed to say, 'Don't spoil our lovely experience, we are still filled with delight of the spirit, don't distract us.'" Thus, the Silence Game came into being.

Playing the Silence Game can give children a sense of joy, achievement, and social spirit as the group works together for a common goal. It also helps children develop a higher level of self-control, which in turn contributes to the normalization of the classroom. In 1930 Montessori wrote that the Silence Game brings "little by little a discipline composed of calmness and inner beatitude." ("The Importance and the Nature of the Silence Game," *AMI Communications*, 1976)

Indirect Preparation

All the exercises in Practical Life, especially the Grace and Courtesy lessons, are indirect preparation for the Silence Game. Children learn to control and perfect their movements: pushing in a chair quietly and carefully, walking around a work rug on the floor, pouring the rice carefully without the sound of even one grain spilling on the table.

These activities help children develop concentration and precision, as well as social awareness, as they wait for their turn, without disturbing the classmate who is working. They learn to speak softly in response to the teacher's quiet voice, and to stop moving and listen when a chime is rung, or the lights are turned off.

Direct Preparation

Here are some games that can be played to help children perfect the ability to listen and to still the body:

1. Pass a bell around the circle, encouraging the children to not let it ring.

2. Invite children to listen to the sound of birds singing or the rain striking the windowpanes.

3. Have the children close their eyes. Then play several familiar instruments (egg shaker, rhythm

sticks, cymbals). Ask them to identify, by the sound, which instrument was played.

4. Invite a small group of children to sit quietly with their eyes closed for a short amount of time (start with 20-30 seconds). Afterwards discuss what sounds they heard.

When Are Children Ready?

The Silence Game is best suited for children ages four and up. It should not be attempted until there is certainty of success, and for many classrooms that may be sometime in the spring after months of preparation. You'll know that the children in your classroom are ready to play the Silence Game when they can:

- Control their movements.

- Sit quietly and listen for a period of time.

- Concentrate and work independently.

- Cooperate with each other.

Don't be discouraged if one or two children aren't able to be quiet enough to participate. Your classroom assistant could work with them on a special project outside the classroom.

Playing the Silence Game

Many teachers first introduce the Silence Game when the whole class is gathered, in order to explain and practice the game. Older children can model how to get up, ever so quietly, and go to the teacher once their name is called.

Some teachers choose to hold up a card during the work period that reads "Silence" and then wait, as one-by-one, the children notice, stop working, and become still and silent. Some teachers encourage the children to close their eyes. Then the teacher goes to a far corner or walks out of the room to whisper the children's names. When a child hears her name, she goes over to the teacher and sits near her.

When all the children have heard their whispered names and come to you, you might want to take them outside for a celebratory walk in the garden. Be creative and vary the activities you do after playing this game: group singing, a birthday celebration, or simply a return to work.

Today we live in a noisy world, filled with the sounds of the television, electronics, phone conversations, leaf blowers, sirens, and traffic. Many of us rarely have the opportunity to experience silence or to savor the quieter sounds of bees buzzing, wind rustling the leaves, or a fire crackling in the fireplace. The Silence Game can give children a precious gift that could last a lifetime: the ability to cultivate and appreciate silence.

Felt Patterning

A pattern is a series of repeated lines or shapes

Preparation: Felt strips with felt shapes arranged in a pattern sequence and glued on.

Supplies: Felt shapes of various colors, and long horizontal felt strips

Lessons- place felt shapes in a jar or small basket. Long horizontal strips are used as the space to place the varying patterns and the child has the opportunity to create her own patterns.

Felt Circles- various sizes and colors

Lesson- we are working on gradation of size so if for example you have a red circle, you need to have red circles of differing sizes. This will introduce language as "small, smaller, smallest" or "larger, largest, etc."

Sandpaper Rubbings- use the metal insets to trace the shapes on sandpaper. Cut them out.

Lesson: Place a sandpaper shape on the table rough side up. Place a paper on top. Rub with the side of a fat crayon

Chalk Board – small chalkboard and chalk. Make lines from left to right. Say "left to right." Fill the board with lines. Erase. Make lines top to bottom. Say "top to bottom." Fill the board with lines, Erase.

Matching Cards- pairs of picture to picture cards to be matched. These are also known as three-part cards. It can be played as partner game and as a matching game with the cards turned upside down.

Parts of a … Nomenclature cards (as Parts of a … Book)

Parts of an object such as "parts of an insect" which are simplified drawing in which a child can break down each part of the simple line drawing. The child will color the specific part of the object one at a time, isolating the part and then the name of the specific part is written on the page. Make sure to make enough copies to accommodate the number of parts.

Matching Letters-make pairs of cards with the lower-case letters s-m-a-t. As each set of letters is introduced, they may be used in combination with previously introduced letter. Sets of letters are: smat, fbox, hnde, cpur, wigl, zkqyv. Mix the letters and match in pairs. It can also be played as a memory game. This will be a great way to utilize sandpaper letters if you have them available.

Name tracing- Make a name card- write or print the child's first and last name on a piece of paper and laminate it. Cut pieces of tracing paper the same size as the card. Two clothespins or paper clips, pencil.

Lesson: Place the paper on the name and clip in place. Trace the name. Use with the sandpaper letters if you have them available to practice how the strokes are done.

Season sorting cards –

Preparation of the work: Find or take pictures of children that match the seasons and give representations of seasons changing. Have at least 4 pictures to represent each season. Make four season cards: a simple leaf drawing with the word "Fall" on the back, snowflake with the word "winter," flower with the word "spring," and sun with the word "summer," – laminate all cards.

Lesson- this is a sorting work to be placed in a basket.

Botany

Leaf Press (can be used for flowers as well)

Materials:

- 1 medium sized corrugated cardboard box

- 12 pieces of printer/copy paper

- Rubber bands (at least 2 thick rubber bands) – extra-large file folder rubber bands work great

- Scissors

- Markers or crayons

- Stickers (optional)

1. Help your child cut out six (6 inches by 6 inches) pieces of cardboard box.

2. Next, cut out twelve (6 inches by 6 inch) pieces of paper.

3. Put the press together by alternating the cardboard and papers.

4. Encourage your child to decorate the top layer with their name, stickers or designs. Then go outside to find some interesting leaves, plants and blossoms.

5. Fill the press by putting leaves and flowers between the paper layers of the press. You may want to add notes on the paper about where and when you found the nature items.

6. Secure your press with the rubber bands. Keep the items in the press for about two weeks.
   Other ideas:

7. – Used recycled newspaper instead of printer paper.

8. – Use a glue stick to glue your dried flowers to construction paper to make bookmarks or cards.

9. – Make a dried flower window display. Preserve your dried flowers in between two pieces of clear contact paper. Cut the contact paper into a circle or trim off the edges to make a neat rectangle or square. Hang your creation in a window or put it on your refrigerator for display.

Using the Lesson Plan in a 3-6-year-old classroom

The Children's House is the core of the Montessori Method and is the curriculum of the 3 – 6-year-old child. These classrooms are the starting place, and mainstay, of Montessori education around the world. Developmentally, children at this age need to explore and discover in order to address their insatiable curiosity. These children possess an <u>Absorbent Mind</u>.

Our early childhood classrooms are specifically designed to stimulate and engage children's senses. Each classroom has two adults: a teacher with a unique role accompanied by an assistant. With careful guidance from their teacher, children have the freedom to work independently based on their interests. MSB's distinctive learning environments are aesthetically inviting with an array of learning materials, plants, animals, art, music and direct access to nature. Specially designed, hands-on materials that engage children in learning are everywhere. When children are provided self-direction, and learn through self-discovery, they cultivate strong characteristics such as motivation, concentration, self-discipline and a genuine love of learning.

Children around the age of 3 begin school in the morning program, ending at 11:30. Once a child is ready to stay for lunch, around the age of 4, they may remain at school until 12:30. Once a child turns 5 they may join the extended day program and are dismissed at 2:45.

A Learning Community

The Children's House is a place where children, 3 –
6 years old, can work at their own tempo and follow their
curiosities without interruption. It is a place where they
can feel at home. Our Early Childhood Program consists
of mixed-age classrooms, taking full advantage of the
crossover within the developmental stage between 3
and 6 years. Children learn to cooperate with children of
different ages and to respect each other's efforts. They
learn to care for themselves, aid others and be
conscious of their environment. The classroom is a
microcosm, a flourishing community where children
display, and are shown, respect and dignity.

An Environment Built for Learning

Above all else, our classrooms are prepared with the
child in mind. The physical space and routines are
harmonized to enhance exploration and independent
learning. The room is set up at child height, enabling
children to reach what they want without relying on
adult help. We believe that children learn more by
direct experience and less by simply listening to an adult
talk. Our specially designed Montessori
materials are simple, elegant and stimulating. They
appeal specifically to the child at this stage of
development. This prepared environment only includes
items that will engage children and encourage
spontaneous activity. Each classroom also has an
equivalent outdoor footprint to enhance children's'
sense of our interconnectedness with nature.

Curriculum

Our daily work in the classroom is clearly defined by a
challenging Montessori curriculum that is composed of:

Art, Botany, Drama, Environmental Studies, Geography, Geometry, Language, Mathematics, Music, Practical Life, Sensorial Activities, Practical Life

The exercises of Practical Life provide the foundation for all other activities in the Montessori classroom, fulfilling the child's plea: "Help me to do it myself!" Through exercises in daily living, such as pouring and scrubbing, sewing and gardening, or practicing grace and courtesy, the child gains confidence and mastery of the environment, after individual skills are refined, children apply them in purposeful work, such as serving juice or polishing. Specifically, these activities contribute to the control and coordination of movement, development of concentration, and the self-esteem that comes with making a real contribution to the group.

Pouring & Transferring

Grasping a handle and pouring water or grains helps children develop fine motor control. These simple activities isolate single skills children will later need, in combination, for more complex processes. One principle behind the activities Montessori designed was that "control of error" be evident. Children learn to correct themselves in their work, eliminating the need for adults to point out mistakes. In this spirit, most of the pitchers and dishes we offer are breakable.

Washing & Cleaning

A basic premise behind Maria Montessori's philosophy of early childhood education was that every child is eager for work, even when the work seems like chores to the adult. Through the activities of Practical Life, children not only perform a task; they are also forming foundations on which to organize skills and intelligence. Nowhere is this premise more evident than in Washing and Scrubbing exercises. Through these activities, children develop concentration, become aware of order and sequencing, gain control over their movements, become more independent, and learn to care for their surroundings.

Polishing

A Primary Montessori classroom without polishing activities would be as dull as tarnished silver! Children feel a sense of accomplishment when they see an object fade behind a coating of polish and then reappear all shiny—after a little rubbing, of course. Polishing activities give children a chance to synthesize preliminary skills, such as making a cotton swab and using an eye dropper, into an orderly sequence that yields such a satisfying result. With plenty of polishing variations on the shelf, your children will be shining all year.

Manipulatives

In *The Secret of Childhood*, Montessori wrote that the human hand… *"not only allows the mind to reveal itself but enables the whole being to enter into special relationships with its environment."* Manipulative activities like these engage hands and eyes in a practical task that satisfies the child's need for purposeful work. At the same time, such activities offer unique physical challenges that help children develop concentration and learn to coordinate their most important "tools": eyes and hands!

Food Preparation

When children begin to internalize the foundations of Practical Life, they seek ways to use their skills and assume broader responsibilities. Preliminary activities that isolate single skills demonstrate children's amazing ability to handle kitchen tools. Preparing and serving snacks (and even meals) is a natural way for children to learn cooperation and experience community. Where kitchen facilities are limited, create cooking and clean-up areas with a toaster oven, cutting boards, basins, and pitchers.

Sensorial

Children from birth to age six are in their "sensitive period" for exploring the world through their senses. Maria Montessori encouraged us to provide children with many opportunities to organize the sensory impressions they've been receiving since birth. By your careful selection of items of different textures, colors, sizes, and geometric shapes, children will discover relationships and exclaim, "This bolt is a hexagon," or "This cloth is rough." Sensorial experiences also indirectly prepare children for future exploration of language, mathematics, geometry, art, and music.

Language

Montessori perceived the miracle of language development as "a treasure prepared in the unconscious, which is then handed over to consciousness, and the child, in full possession of his new power, talks and talks without cessation."

Absorbing and perfecting language depends on human contact, but language is not taught. Words are the labels for our experiences. A child who has varied experiences and is given the words for those experiences will develop a well-rounded means of expression. Just as a rich vocabulary is dependent on the child's experience, the transition to reading and writing is dependent on a strong vocabulary. Soon, the child, explorer of the world, will be able to express thoughts and understand and interpret the thoughts of others.

Math

We are providing you with an overview of the Primary Montessori Math Program so that you have a better overall picture of the progression of materials and lessons.

Math is logic, sequence, order, and the extrapolation of truth. In the Montessori philosophy it's stated that the child has a 'mathematical mind' and an internal drive to understand the environment around them. It can therefore be said that children have an inborn attraction for math. Their minds are full of energy that propels them to absorb, manipulate, classify, order, sequence, abstract, and repeat. These tendencies are those which help the child to acquire a greater depth to his mathematical knowledge.

It is the precision of the presentations and the exactness of the math materials that attract children to this area of the classroom. As well, children in the primary Montessori classroom are in the process (sensitive period) of fine tuning their perceptions. Children are sensitive to minute changes in order, sequence, and size. They will notice a teeny tiny bug in the crack of the sidewalk where as adults will walk by blindly without notice.

The exercises in the math area offer the children the 'keys' that they will need to send them on the road to further exploration and maturation of the mathematical mind. The ways in which the materials are ordered allows the children to complete full intellectual cycles that help them to achieve the freedom to become independent.

Math in the primary classroom is made up of many little details that form a whole, but each detail is complete unto itself. All early math exercises are worked at the sensorial level to ensure that the child relates the quantity to the symbol (example: Spindle Boxes).

Botany

Botany studies begin with a look at the life cycle of plants and presentations which explore the importance of plants to human and animal life. Students are encouraged to look at the many ways that plants provide for our fundamental needs. They do this with a variety of independent research projects. Botany studies continue with presentations of nomenclature and impressionistic charts which detail the basic needs of plants, their parts, and the functions of these parts. Students study roots, stems, leaves, flowers and fruits. They learn about plant reproduction, pollination, phyllotaxis, photosynthesis, monocotyledons and dicotyledons, succulent and dehiscent fruits, seeds and the means by which they travel, and alternate means of regenerating. They learn about the system of scientific classification with materials such as the Five Kingdoms Chart and the Plant Classification Chart.

All botany studies are supported by experiments that illustrate how the plant meets its needs, how plant systems function, and the importance of plants to the ecosystem. Students are actively involved in growing, caring for and observing plants in the classroom. Botany work also parallels studies in geography, history and zoology that explore the role of plants on Earth. It is our goal that the children understand, from these studies, the interdependence of all life forms and the custodial role humans must assume to protect and preserve life on Earth.

Geography

One of the many gifts a Montessori education often brings is a life-long enthusiasm for geography. Geography helps children place themselves on Earth, fostering care for the rivers, forests, oceans, and peoples. Physical geography focuses on the features of Earth's environment. Political geography studies how humans have adapted to the land, emphasizing settlement and activity.

Geography is the most all-encompassing subject in the Montessori "cultural curriculum." It creates the foundation for understanding the oneness of the human family, recognizing the basic needs that all people share while appreciating the diversity of how different cultures satisfy those same needs.

Physical and Political Geography

We begin with physical geography, introducing three- and four-year-olds to the Globe of Land and Water (Sandpaper Globe). The sandpaper land is rough to the touch; the oceans are smooth. *"This is how we see Earth from the sky. This is land. This is water."*

We also introduce children to Land and Water Forms, a Practical Life exercise in geography. As the child pours water into the forms, she has the sensorial impression of, for example, an island and a lake. Naming the landforms using three-part cards and learning the definitions of landforms follow.

The materials in the primary classroom for political geography include the Globe of the Continents (Painted Globe) and the Puzzle Map of the World (typically introduced as a sensorial work), along with the Continent Maps, outline maps, and the flags.

Introducing Maps

Once children have worked with the globes, we introduce maps. This transition from globe to map is often difficult for a child. You can compare the Globe of the Continents to the Puzzle Map of the World, identifying each continent on the globe, then the map. You could say, "A map is an important tool to show what a big place looks like from up high." Perhaps you could demonstrate how to make a flat map of the spherical world by letting the air out of an inflatable globe to flatten it. Then compare it to the Puzzle Map of the World.

Five- to nine-year-olds might enjoy drawing maps of their school playground, the lizard's terrarium, or the route from home to school. A treasure map leading to a hidden command card or object in the classroom can encourage map-reading skills.

Exploring the Continents

Most teachers spend hours researching and gathering artifacts to present the physical and political geography of each continent in turn. Storytelling and photographs can bring the countries and continents to life as we introduce children to:

- three-part cards of the people, landmarks, flora, and fauna.

- climates and biomes. Discuss how these affect the clothing people wear and the foods they eat.

- languages, songs, stories, religions, holidays, and foods. Invite parents with knowledge of another country to share their culture.

- artwork, clothing, and instruments.

- physical and political maps.

- the significance of the colors and symbols on flags. Children can make and color flags.

MY BIO

Hello! My name is Robin Norgren and I feel honored to be a part of the Montessori community. I come with almost 20 years' experience in management and a love of education and creativity and believe that lifelong learning is key to navigating the world we live in.

I was born in Wurzburg, Germany where my dad was stationed with the U.S. Army. I spent most of my childhood in Detroit, Michigan but moved to Arizona when I was 14 years old.
I have been married for 16 years and my husband has proudly served in the U.S. Navy for almost 20 years, so I have been privileged to have traveled quite a bit. I have two children, a boy and a girl ages 29 and 12. The oldest

is in the U.S. Air Force and currently stationed in North Korea and the youngest is excited to start Junior High.

I attended Arizona State University and earned my Bachelor of Science degree in business management and worked in retail for about 15 years and really enjoyed mentoring and training young employees not just about work but life.

When I met my husband, we had dreams of being in the military together which is why I attended Fuller Theological Seminary and earned my degree in Theology with aspirations of becoming a chaplain. But God had other plans and weeks after my candidate packet was rejected, we found out we were pregnant with our youngest. Due to the world's political climate during that time, we decided to rethink how our family would move forward since he was beginning to be deployed for long periods of time. I had a friend who talked highly about Montessori with me throughout the years so I investigated it further and decided this might be a beautiful next step.

I began my AMI certification and unfortunately had to put it on hold when my husband was reassigned to Virginia, so I took my AMS certification and completed it in 2016. I am still in the process of completing my AMI certification because I find both offer a deep and rich understanding of Montessori not simply as an education process but as a lifestyle and a worldview.

I also am passionate about art education and have created programs that I have taught in both Arizona and Virginia to pre-k to 6th grade classrooms. Because I have worked in a Reggio Emilio school, I have a working knowledge of creating an Atelier space within the classroom. I have a passion for not only inspiring children to be lifelong learners but modeling it as well.

I commit to be a teacher who offers your children not only a vibrant education but an opportunity to build confidence and become independent individuals who are mindful of the world around them and interested in learning and growing into the peacemakers and change agents the world needs.

Robin Norgren, M.A.
M.A. Theology, Fuller Theological Seminary
B.S. Management, Arizona State University
A.M.S. Primary Certification, KHT Montessori
A.M.I. Primary Certification Candidate, S.I.M.S.
Life Coaching Certification, S.W.I.H.A.

CLICK HERE to view my freebies

CLICK HERE to view my drawing lessons

CLICK HERE to view my Art with the Masters projects

CLICK HERE to view my Contemporary Artist lessons

CLICK HERE to view art lessons that go along with popular books

CLICK HERE to view my self-esteem projects

CLICK HERE to view my class mural ideas

CLICK HERE to view my fun art folk art lessons

CLICK HERE to view 3 Bundled Lessons

CLICK HERE to view 5 Bundled lessons

CLICK HERE to check my reviews

OR

ORDER DIRECTLY FROM ME!

http://www.brightchildmontessori.com

is where you will find all my lesson plans and supplemental materials to make your Montessori Experience an enjoyable one

Made in the USA
Monee, IL
02 July 2023

38406243R00073